扫描文章前的二维码
收听该故事的英文音频

"伟人的少年故事"丛书

双语读物

迷人的科学

—— 用思想创造奇迹的科学家 ——

（斯里兰卡）努雷·维塔奇（Nury Vittachi） 著
斯泰帕·张（Step Cheung） 图
朱之翀 译　张群 审校

上海科技教育出版社

World Scientific
Connecting Great Minds

图书在版编目(CIP)数据

迷人的科学：用思想创造奇迹的科学家/（斯里）努雷·维塔奇（Nury Vittachi）著；朱之翀译.—上海：上海科技教育出版社，2018.8

（"伟人的少年故事"丛书）

书名原文：Magical Mathematics

ISBN 978-7-5428-6712-4

Ⅰ.①迷… Ⅱ.①努… ②朱… Ⅲ.①科学家—生平事迹—世界—青少年读物 Ⅳ.① K816.11—49

中国版本图书馆 CIP 数据核字（2018）第 069157 号

Contents

Lilavati The Girl, the Pearl and the Not-so-sad Story 2

Carl Gauss The Boy with No Birthday 13

Philippa Garrett The Math Girl Who Stunned the World 21

Srinivasa Ramanujan The Penniless Youth Who Amazed the Professors 30

Maria Agnesi The Good Witch Who Made an Amazing Decision 39

F.F. Runge The Strange Adventures of Dr. Poison 47

Rosalind Franklin The Young Woman Who Was Forgotten 55

Alessandra Giliani The Girl in the Chamber of Corpses 63

Alice Evans The Farm Girl Who Made Your Milk Safe 70

Frank Epperson A Tasty Treat Found by Accident 78

目 录

莉拉瓦蒂 女孩、珍珠和不太糟的故事 2

卡尔·弗雷德里希·高斯 没有生日的男孩 13

菲丽帕·福西特 震惊全球的数学女孩 21

斯里尼瓦瑟·拉马努金 震惊教授的穷小子 30

玛丽亚·阿涅西 作出惊人决定的女巫 39

弗里德莱布·斐迪南·朗格 毒药博士的奇幻冒险 47

罗莎琳德·富兰克林 被遗忘的年轻女子 55

亚历山德拉·吉莉安 停尸房里的女孩 63

爱丽丝·凯瑟琳·埃文斯 保证牛奶安全的农场姑娘 70

弗兰克·埃珀森 偶然发现的美味食品 78

THE GIRL, THE PEARL AND THE NOT-SO-SAD STORY

莉拉瓦蒂
女孩、珍珠和不太糟的故事

ONE BRIGHT DAY MORE than 900 years ago, a girl and her father sat in the shade of a tree with a pen and paper. They were playing thinking games.

Her **nickname**[①] was Lilavati, which meant little Miss Playful.

His name was Bhaskara and he was a professional wise man, a heaven-watching advisor to the rulers.

Their favorite game was mathematics magic: they sat for hours experimenting with numbers, discovering **astonishing**[②] hidden patterns and surprise answers. Playing this sort of game, Lilavati realized, was fun but it was also amazing exercise for the brain.

Every sunset, after Lilavati went to sleep, Bhaskara went to work, for **stargazing**[③] was one of his most important jobs.

From the dawn of time, people have looked to the heavens when thinking about big ideas. Although these days we make a clear difference between astronomers and **astrologers**[④], in the past, these ideas were all mixed together. There was no such word as "scientist" until 1832. Instead, for most of recorded history, there were people called **Natural Philosophers**[⑤], who looked at the world around them and tried to understand it.

900多年前的一天,天气晴朗,一个小女孩和父亲一起坐在树荫下。他们拿着纸和笔,在玩思维游戏。

女孩的小名叫莉拉瓦蒂(Lilavati),意思是热爱嬉戏的小姑娘。

她的父亲名叫婆什迦罗(Bhaskara),是一位非常博学的男子。他专门观察天象,是统治者的天象顾问。

莉拉瓦蒂和父亲两人最喜欢玩的游戏就是数学魔术:他们可以一坐几小时,用数字做实验,发现数字背后所隐藏的令人惊讶的模式与答案。莉拉瓦蒂发现,玩这类游戏很有趣,同时对大脑来说也是很好的锻炼。

每天,当太阳下山、莉拉瓦蒂入睡之后,婆什迦罗开始工作。他最重要的工作之一就是眺望星空。

从远古时代开始,人们沉思时就会眺望天空。尽管现在我们已经明确地将天文学家和占星家区分开来,但在古代,这两个概念是混在一起的。直到1832年,"科学家"这个词才被发明出来。在大部分有文字记载的历史时期,有一些人被称为自然哲学家,他们观察身处的这个世界并且尽力去弄清它。

① **nickname** ['nɪkneɪm] *n.* 绰号、昵称;*vt.* 给……取绰号 [nicknamed, nicknamed, nicknaming]
② **astonishing** [ə'stɒnɪʃɪŋ] *adj.* 惊人的、令人惊讶的;*v.* 使……惊讶, 使……诧异
③ **stargaze** ['stɑːgeɪz] *vi.* 耽于幻想、眺望星辰 [stargazed, stargazed, stargazing]
④ **astrologer** [ə'strɒlədʒə] *n.* 占星家
⑤ **natural philosopher** 自然哲学家

One day, Bhaskara's stargazer colleagues came to him with some bad news. They said his daughter's star charts predicted that she would not get married or have children.

What could the stargazer do? He knew it was possible for a person to live a happy life without a **spouse**① or children — but he had always felt that Lilavati was destined to be remembered. But who would remember her if she had no offspring?

That night he looked up at stars with his daughter in mind, and considered all the forms of knowledge he could find, from natural philosophy to beliefs about birthdays. Ancient ideas about "**auspicious**② moments" suggested that there was one chance for her to change her destiny.

He got the feeling that if Lilavati chose by herself to get married at one particular time, she might avoid the bad fortune of not having a family. To be childless was considered a sad state of affairs for a woman at that time and in that place: India in the 1100s.

So Bhaskara set to work. He **constructed**③ a machine in which water would flow slowly from one part to another, working as a type of clock, to tell the girl when to get married.

He would step away from the house, but the water clock would tell her the right moment.

"Don't go near it," Bhaskara told Lilavati. "Just wait for a signal."

有一天，婆什迦罗的占星家同事告诉他一个坏消息，说他女儿的星象预示着她可能不会结婚，也没有孩子。

这位占星家怎么办呢？婆什迦罗知道，没有配偶和孩子的人一生也可能过得快乐幸福——但他总觉得莉拉瓦蒂注定要被人们所铭记。可如果她没有后代的话，谁会记得她呢？

那一夜，他想着女儿，抬头仰望星空，思忖着自己所掌握的所有知识体系——从自然哲学到诞辰信仰。古代关于"吉兆"的思想，表明她有一个改变命运的机会。

婆什迦罗有一个预感：如果莉拉瓦蒂在他所选择的一个特定时间点上结婚，她可能就能避开坏运气，组建家庭。在 12 世纪的印度，女性没有后代被认为是一件不幸的事。

婆什迦罗开始认真工作。他制造了一台机器，可以让水缓缓地从一个部位流向另一个部位，就像钟一样运转，以此来告诉女孩什么时候结婚。

他将要离家外出，不过水钟会告诉莉拉瓦蒂那个恰当的结婚时间点。

"不要靠近它，"婆什迦罗对莉拉瓦蒂说，"等待信号就好。"

---

① **spouse** [spaʊz; -s] *n.* 配偶；*vt.* 和……结婚 [spoused, spoused, spousing]
② **auspicious** [ɔːˈspɪʃəs] *adj.* 吉兆的、吉利的、幸运的
③ **construct** [kənˈstrʌkt] *vt.* 建造、构造、创立；*n.* 构想、概念

Then he left her alone.

Sitting in her wedding dress, Lilavati waited.

And waited.

And waited.

Then she tiptoed over and **peered**[1] at the machine. A pearl from her headdress fell into the water — and stopped the machine working.

But Lilavati did not notice.

The auspicious moment passed. And the signal was not given.

Some historians say she missed the right time and decided not to marry. Others say she did get married but at the wrong hour, and her husband died within days, leaving her a young, childless widow.

Whichever it was, we do know that she never became a wife and mother.

Instead, she and her beloved father found themselves together again, both feeling really sad.

But then she had an idea. She got out a piece of paper and a pen and they started playing mathematics games again.

Their smiles returned.

And then Bhaskara decided to **capture**[2] their games on paper.

A book was published in AD 1150. It was a mathematics textbook, but it was not called "Mathematics Textbook" and it was not filled with exercises.

然后他就离开了,留下莉拉瓦蒂一个人。

莉拉瓦蒂身穿嫁衣,坐着等待着那个时刻的到来。

她等待着。

等待着。

过了一阵,她蹑手蹑脚地走近机器,盯着它看。这时她头饰上的一颗珍珠掉进水里——机器停止运转了。

但莉拉瓦蒂没有发现。

吉时已过,机器并没有给出信号。

一些历史学家说,她错过了时间,决定不再结婚。其他历史学家则说她结婚了,但时机不对,没几天她的丈夫就去世了,她成了一名没有孩子的年轻寡妇。

无论是哪种情况,她都没能成为妻子、母亲。这是不争的事实。

她与亲爱的父亲重逢了,两个人都感到非常难过。

但她想出了一个办法。她拿出一支笔和一张纸,两人再一次玩起了数学游戏。

他们的脸上重新洋溢起了笑容。

后来,婆什迦罗决定把他们玩的游戏记录在纸上。

1150 年时,一本书出版了。这是一本数学教科书,但书名不叫"数学教科书",书上也没有习题。

---

① **peer**［pɪə］*vi.* 凝视、盯着看,窥视

② **capture**［ˈkæptʃə］*vt.* 俘获、夺得、捕捉、拍摄、录制;*n.* 捕获、战利品、俘虏

No. It was called "Lilavati" and was filled with **conversations**[1] about numbers. It said things like: "**Fawn**[2]-eyed child Lilavati, what is 135 **multiplied**[3] by 12, beautiful one?"

The book became one of the top mathematics books in the world. It was used for centuries and taught countless numbers of children the joy of numbers.

Lilavati's friends, who got married and had children in the normal way, have all been forgotten. But nine centuries later, the girl whose love of numbers inspired **numerous**[4] generations is still remembered.

这本书叫"莉拉瓦蒂",书中的内容都是与数字计算有关的对话。例如:"美丽的小孩,浅褐色眼睛的莉拉瓦蒂,135 乘以 12 是多少呀?"

这本书成为世界最受欢迎的数学书之一,被使用了数百年,向不计其数的小朋友传授了数学的乐趣。

莉拉瓦蒂的朋友,那些像正常人一样结婚生子的都被忘记了。但莉拉瓦蒂,这个以其对数字的爱激励了一代又一代人的女孩,在 900 年后依旧活在人们的心中。

....

① **conversation** [ˌkɒnvəˈseɪʃ(ə)n] n. 交谈、会话,社交、交往、交际,会谈、(人与计算机的)人机对话

② **fawn** [fɔːn] adj. 浅黄褐色的

③ **multiply** [ˈmʌltɪplaɪ] vt. 乘、使增加、使相乘、使繁殖;vi. 乘、繁殖、增加;adv. 多样地、复合地;adj. 多层的、多样的 [multiplied, multiplied, multiplying]

④ **numerous** [ˈnjuːm(ə)rəs] adj. 许多的、很多的 [more numerous, most numerous]

THE BOY WITH NO BIRTHDAY

卡尔·弗雷德里希·高斯
没有生日的男孩

ONCE UPON A TIME, there was a boy with no birthday. Carl Gauss had been born on a particular day, just like the rest of us, but no one knew what it was.

His mother was very poor and **illiterate**①, which meant that she could not read or write, so she hadn't written it down.

"It was a Wednesday," she would say. And she would mention a particular church **ritual**②. "And it was eight days before the **Feast of Ascension**③."

His father was poor, too, working outdoors as a gardener and **bricklayer**④ in Germany.

But his mother wanted her son to be successful, so she encouraged him to learn writing and mathematics.

One day, when Carl was three years old, he saw his father working on a **payroll**⑤ calculation.

"You made a mistake," the boy said, pointing it out. "And I can tell you what the right answer should be."

His father was **stunned**⑥: his sums were being corrected by a child who was little more than a toddler.

When he was seven, Carl was sent to school. One day, his teacher set his students a challenge: add up all the numbers between 1 and 100 and write down the answer.

很久以前，有一个没有生日的男孩。像其他人一样，卡尔·弗雷德里希·高斯（Carl Friedrich Gauss）出生于某一天，但没人知道是哪一天。

他的母亲非常穷，没有受过教育，她不会读书写字，所以没有把那一天记录下来。

"那是个星期三。"她只能说出这些。同时，她提到了一个特殊的宗教纪念日："那是在耶稣升天节的 8 天前。"

他的父亲也很穷，是德国的一个户外园丁与砖匠。

但母亲希望孩子出人头地，所以她鼓励卡尔学习写字和数学。

卡尔三岁的一天，他看见父亲在计算工资。

"你算错了，"男孩对父亲说，并指出了那个错误，"让我来告诉你正确答案是多少。"

父亲十分惊讶：他计算出来的数额竟然让一个蹒跚学步的孩子纠正了！

卡尔 7 岁时，他被送到学校读书。一天，老师给学生布置了一道难题：计算从 1 到 100 的所有数之和，并写下答案。

---

① **illiterate** [ɪˈlɪt(ə)rət] *adj.* 文盲的、不识字的、没受教育的；*n.* 文盲
② **ritual** [ˈrɪtʃuəl] *n.* 仪式、惯例、礼制；*adj.* 仪式的、例行的、礼节性的
③ **Feast of Ascension** 耶稣升天节
④ **bricklayer** [ˈbrɪkleɪə] *n.* 砖匠
⑤ **payroll** [ˈpeɪrəʊl] *n.* 工资单、在册职工人数、工资名单
⑥ **stunned** [stʌn] *v.* 使震惊、使不知所措 [stunned, stunned]

Everyone started doing the sums.

But not Carl.

Was it too hard for him?

No, quite the **opposite**[1]. He told his teacher: "I don't need to add them up. It would obviously be 50 pairs of numbers each totaling 101, so that would be 5,050, right?"

He was right.

The school and his parents realized that they had a **genuine**[2] **genius**[3] on their hands. Carl Friedrich Gauss quickly became **recognized**[4] as one of the greatest mathematicians in history, even while he was just a teenager. Here are some examples of his influence.

1) When Carl Gauss was 19, he managed to solve a math puzzle that had **baffled**[5] the ancient Greek thinkers, whose wisdom was **legendary**[6].

每个人都开始计算。

除了卡尔。

这对于他来说是不是太难了？

不，恰恰相反。他告诉老师："我不需要把它们一个个加起来。1 到 100 明显是 50 组数，而每一组两个数加起来的和都是 101，所以答案是 5050。对吗？"

他的答案是正确的。

他的父母和学校都意识到，卡尔是一位真正的神童。尽管当时还只是一名少年，卡尔·弗雷德里希·高斯很快就被认为是历史上最伟大的数学家之一。以下是一些有关他影响的例子：

1. 19 岁时，高斯成功地解决了长期困扰古希腊学者的一个数学谜题，这些学者是传说中智慧过人的智者。

① **opposite** [ˈɒpəzɪt; -sɪt] *adj.* 相反的、对面的、对立的；*n.* 对立面、反义词；*prep.* 在……的对面；*adv.* 在对面
② **genuine** [ˈdʒenjʊɪn] *adj.* 真实的、真正的，诚恳的 [more genuine, most genuine]
③ **genius** [ˈdʒiːnɪəs] *n.* 天才、天赋，精神
④ **recognize** [ˈrekəɡnaɪz] *vt.* 认出、识别、承认；*vi.* 确认、承认，具结 [recognized, recognized, recognizing]
⑤ **baffle** [ˈbæf(ə)l] *vt.* 使……困惑、使……受挫折，用挡板控制；*n.* 挡板、困惑；*vi.* 做徒劳挣扎 [baffled, baffled, baffling]
⑥ **legendary** [ˈledʒ(ə)nd(ə)rɪ] *adj.* 传说的、传奇的；*n.* 传说集、圣徒传 [legendaries]

2) He used math to find a lost planet. An astronomer named Giuseppe Piazzi discovered a small planet which he called Ceres. But it seemed to move oddly, and one day it totally disappeared.

Carl asked to look at the data that Piazzi had written down about where and when he had seen the planet Ceres.

The young man then did some math and worked out exactly when and where Ceres would reappear in the night sky — and he turned out to be exactly right.

3) Even today, people use his mathematics to help them. When the technology experts who made the famous software program Adobe Photoshop wanted a way to teach computers to use mathematics to make perfectly soft, fuzzy colors — **randomized**[1], but with no **blotchy**[2] bits — they used Gauss's math to produce a popular photo-editing option called **Gaussian Blur**[3].

But best of all, Carl used mathematics to solve the puzzle of his own birthday. By using the clues his mother had given him about the day of the week and the church ritual, he calculated that he was born on Wednesday, April 30, 1777.

At last he knew when to celebrate. Happy birthday, Carl!

2. 他用数学方法找到了一颗失落的星球。一位名叫皮亚齐（Giuseppe Piazzi）的天文学家发现了一颗小的行星，他称之为谷神星。但这颗谷神星运行起来很没有规律，某一天它甚至彻底消失了。

卡尔请求查看皮亚齐的记录，他所观察到的有关谷神星出现时间与位置的数据。

接着，卡尔进行了一些数学运算，得出了谷神星在夜空中将再次出现的确切时间和位置——他的推论后来被证实是正确的。

3. 即使是在当今世界，人们依然受益于卡尔的数学才能。当发明著名的 Adobe Photoshop 软件的科技专家想要让电脑运用数学来营造出随机、柔光、失真但没有污点的颜色时，他们就使用了高斯的数学方法，创建了一种名为"高斯模糊"的著名图片编辑选项。

最棒的是，高斯运用数学算出了自己的生日。通过母亲提供的关于日期和宗教纪念日的线索，他计算出自己的生日是 1777 年 4 月 30 日，星期三。

他终于知道应该在哪一天庆祝自己的生日了。卡尔，生日快乐！

① **randomize** [ˈrændəmaɪz] *vt.* 使随机化、(使)作任意排列或不规则分布 [randomized, randomized, randomizing]

② **blotchy** [ˈblɒtʃɪ] *adj.* 到处有污点的、有疤的 [blotchier, blotchiest]

③ **Gaussian Blur** 高斯模糊（一种滤镜效果）

THE MATH GIRL WHO STUNNED THE WORLD

菲丽帕·福西特
震惊全球的数学女孩

ELIZABETH AND MILLICENT GARRETT were two adult sisters who **campaigned**① for women's rights.

This was in the late 1800s. Men would sometimes **grudgingly**② allow women to play small roles in society "as long as they didn't get in the way".

But the sisters felt this was not good enough. They felt women were as clever as men, and could even be smarter: a claim that made their male friends laugh.

Yet the sisters' own lives showed the truth of their **claims**③.

Elizabeth became the first female registered doctor and surgeon in the UK. Millicent became a famous campaigner in the fight to give women the right to vote.

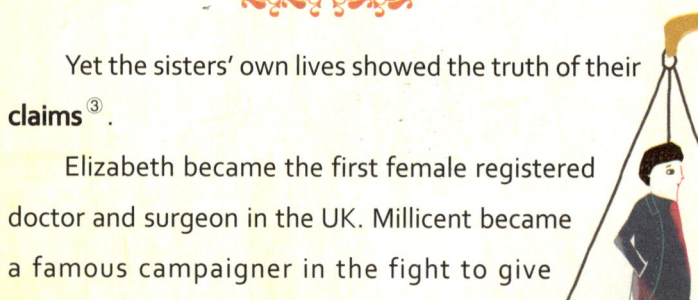

伊丽莎白和米利森特·加勒特（Elizabeth & Millicent Garrett）是为女权奋斗的两位成年姐妹。

故事发生在 19 世纪末。当时的男人们认为，只要女人不妨碍他们，他们允许女人在社会中担任一些小角色，虽然他们并不很情愿。

但这对姐妹认为这样做还远远不够。她们认为女性和男性一样聪明，甚至比一些男性更聪明——听到这样的话，她们的男性朋友都哈哈大笑。

然而这对姐妹的生活证明她们说的是正确的。伊丽莎白后来成为英国第一位女性注册医师兼外科医生。米利森特则成为一位著名的女权运动家，为女性获得投票权而奋斗。

这些成就让人们开始关注平等对待女性的问题，但男性评论家认为，她俩并没有真正地证明女性可以比男性更聪明。

① **campaign** [kæmˈpeɪn] *vi.* 作战、参加竞选、参加活动；*n.* 运动、活动、战役
② **grudgingly** [ˈɡrʌdʒɪŋli] *adv.* 勉强地、不情愿地
③ **claim** [kleɪm] *vi.* 提出要求；*vt.* 要求、声称、需要、认领；*n.* 要求、声称、索赔、断言、值得

These achievements focused on women being treated fairly. But their male **critics**① pointed out that they didn't actually prove that women could be smarter than men.

❧❧ ❦❦

Meanwhile, the two sisters were happy to note that Millicent's teenage daughter Philippa was clearly super-smart, like the other female members of the family.

The high-achieving Garretts helped set up a college in Cambridge. When Philippa was in her late teens, she was allowed to listen to lectures, although only men were allowed to graduate.

❧❧ ❦❦

Cambridge offered a famous test called the **Mathematical Tripos**②, said to be the hardest **undergraduate**③ exam in the world.

Only a small number of men every year entered it. The men who got first class passes were given the title "**wrangler**④" (which means someone who can handle a really tough problem). Some of the world's top scientists and thinkers had started their careers by becoming wranglers at Cambridge.

Every year, the professor who announced the results would take off his hat when he read the top scorer's name, because it was so difficult to win that spot. That man would be given the title senior wrangler, and people assumed that he would become rich and powerful. (The youngest man ever to win the title of senior wrangler went on to become Prime Minister of Great Britain at the age of 24!)

这时，这对姐妹高兴地发现，米利森特的女儿菲丽帕（Philippa）极其聪明，就像这个家庭中的其他女性一样。

成就卓著的加勒特姐妹资助建起了剑桥的一所学院，当菲丽帕快20岁时，她获准去大学旁听，尽管只有男性才能拿到毕业证书。

剑桥大学有一项著名的数学荣誉学位考试，据说是世界上最难的本科生考试。

每年只有少数男生能通过这项考试。以头等成绩通过的男性被称为"优胜者"（表示这是一些能够解决真正难题的人）。世界上一些一流的科学家和思想家，就是在剑桥大学取得"优胜者"称号之后，开始他们的职业生涯的。

每年，宣布考试结果的教授在念到最高分考生的名字时，都会脱下帽子（致敬），因为要赢得这个荣誉太难了。那名考生将被授予"高级优胜者"的称号，人们认为他不久将会成为富豪或权贵。（历史上获得"高级优胜者"称号的最年轻的男子，在24岁时成为英国的首相！）

---

① **critic** [ˈkrɪtɪk] *n.* 批评家、评论家，爱挑剔的人
② **Mathematical Tripos** （剑桥大学）数学荣誉学位考试
③ **undergraduate** [ˌʌndəˈɡrædjuət] *n.* 大学生、大学肄业生；*adj.* 大学生的
④ **wrangler** [ˈræŋɡlə] *n.* 辩论者、争吵者、尤指好辩论者；（剑桥大学）数学荣誉学位考试优胜者

Women were allowed to take the test, just for fun, but of course could not be on the list of wranglers — those titles were for men only.

When Philippa took the test in 1890, she did her very best, wanting to at least get the same score as some of the young men on the list. It would be brilliant if she got the same score as one of the boys in the top ten.

The list of men who had passed the test was read out, and when a certain young male was named, the chief professor removed his hat. A new senior wrangler had been named!

There was loud applause.

But there was a surprise to come. He then read out the list of women who had passed the test that year.

And he announced that Philippa's result was "above the senior wrangler".

Everyone was stunned. She'd beaten ALL the men.

Over the next few days, Philippa's name was in newspapers around the world.

作为娱乐，女性也可以参加这项考试，当然，她们不会出现在优胜者名单中——这项提名只属于男性。

❈❈❈

菲丽帕在1890年参加了这项考试，她竭尽全力，希望取得至少和名单上部分男生一样的分数。如果她能取得和名单上排名第十的男生一样的分数，就可以证明她很杰出了。

通过考试的男生的名字被逐一报出。念到一位年轻男子的名字时，主考官脱下了帽子。一名新的"高级优胜者"诞生了！

掌声雷动。

但接下来发生的一件事更令人惊奇。主考官接着公布了当年通过考试的女性名单。

他宣布：菲丽帕的成绩比"高级优胜者"还要高！

每个人都无比震惊。菲丽帕打败了所有男性！

❈❈❈

在接下来的一段日子里，菲丽帕的名字通过报纸传遍了全世界。

"Once again has woman demonstrated her **superiority**[1] in the face of an **incredulous**[2] and somewhat unsympathetic world," the Daily Telegraph reported on its front page. "And now the last trench has been carried by **Amazonian**[3] **assault**[4], and the whole **citadel**[5] of learning lies open and defenceless…"

Philippa Fawcett worked as a scholar all her life. In May 1948, the Royal Family of the UK passed a **decree**[6] that women could from now on graduate from Cambridge. Philippa, who was then 80 years old, was delighted. She died a month later.

"女性再一次向充满怀疑甚至有些无情的世界展示了自己的卓越，"《每日电讯报》在头版这样写道，"如今，最后一道战壕已被阿玛宗族女战士摧毁，整座学术殿堂都将敞开大门，不再设防……"

菲丽帕·福西特（Philippa Fawcett）终生都是一位学者。1948年的5月，英国皇室通过一条法令，宣布女性从此可以获得剑桥大学毕业证书。已经80高龄的菲丽帕听到这个消息后非常高兴。一个月后，她离开了人世。

① **superiority** [suːˌpɪərɪˈɒrɪtɪ; sjuː-] *n.* 优越、优势、优越性
② **incredulous** [ɪnˈkredjʊləs] *adj.* 怀疑的、不轻信的
③ **amazonian** [ˌæməˈzəʊnjən] *adj.* （希腊神话）阿玛宗族女战士（般）的、亚马孙族女战士（般）的，（女子）尚武善战的、刚勇好战的、骁勇的、强悍的、有男子气概的，（南美洲）亚马孙河的；亚马孙河流域（国家）的；*n.* 亚马孙河地区的印第安人（或居民）
④ **assault** [əˈsɔːlt; əˈsɒlt] *n.* 攻击、袭击；*vt.* 攻击、袭击；*vi.* 袭击、动武
⑤ **citadel** [ˈsɪtəd(ə)l; -del] *n.* 城堡、大本营、避难处
⑥ **decree** [dɪˈkriː] *n.* 法令、判决；*vt.* 命令、颁布、注定、判决；*vi.* 注定、发布命令 [decreed, decreed, decreeing]

THE PENNILESS YOUTH WHO AMAZED THE PROFESSORS

斯里尼瓦瑟·拉马努金
震惊教授的穷小子

WHAT WOULD HAPPEN IF you took the brain of one of the greatest geniuses who ever lived, and put it in the head of a **penniless**①, **starving**② boy in one of the poorest parts of Asia?

Well, it seems that God or Destiny or Fate once did exactly that.

Teenager Srinivasa Ramanujan was so poor that he could not afford the cheapest food in the cheapest shop.

The year was 1906, and he lived in India, in the area known as Madras. At 18 years old, he was starving so badly that he almost died.

He had to beg his friends to give him something to eat and a place to sleep. And then he went knocking on doors in Madras city to see if he could find a job as a lowly clerk in an office. He had no **qualifications**③ or work experience to offer.

The only thing he knew for sure was that he was good at maths — he had won several mathematics prizes when he had been a child at school, in happier times.

He managed to stay alive into his early 20s, and tried to get a job at the tax office. There he met a tax man who loved math and had started the Indian Mathematical Society.

"I can do maths," said Ramanujan. "Look at my notebooks."

如果把有史以来最伟大的天才之一的大脑放进亚洲最贫穷国家的一个饥寒交迫的男孩的头颅里，会发生什么？

上帝或命运似乎这么做过。

一个名叫斯里尼瓦瑟·拉马努金（Srinivasa Ramanujan）的年轻人非常贫穷，连最廉价商店里最便宜的食物都买不起。

那是1906年，这个年轻人住在印度的马德拉斯市（现在的金奈市）。18岁的他饿得快要死了。

他不得不求助朋友，给他一点吃的和一个睡觉的地方。他敲开马德拉斯市一家又一家办公室的大门，想要找到一份卑微的职员工作，然而他没有任何的工作资质或工作经验。

他很清楚，他唯一擅长的就是数学。还是个孩子的时候，他就在学校获得过多个数学奖项，那是一段开心的岁月。

他设法活到了20多岁，试着去一个税务局寻找工作。在那里，他遇到了一位喜爱数学的税务官，这位税务官曾创立了印度数学会。

"我可以做数学方面的工作，"拉马努金说，"看看我的笔记本。"

---

① **penniless** [ˈpɛnɪləs] *adj.* 身无分文的、贫穷的
② **starve** [stɑːv] *v.* 挨饿、使饿死
③ **qualification** [ˌkwɒlɪfɪˈkeɪʃ(ə)n] *n.* 资格、条件、限制、赋予资格

The tax officer looked at the notebooks and realized that the young man was not just good at maths, but astonishingly brilliant. The number puzzles the young man was experimenting with were the sort of thing that top mathematicians played with.

If an uneducated person, who until recently had been little more than a beggar, could do this in his head without training, he must have an astonishing brain.

Instead of giving him a job in the tax office, the man **recommended**[①] that Ramanujan write articles about mathematics for research journals.

But the young man also had to earn money to live, so Ramanujan did that in his spare time while he struggled with lowly jobs. This carried on for years, until another helpful man decided to send the young man's **extraordinary**[②] **equations**[③] to what he felt was the cleverest place on earth — Cambridge University in the UK.

The first two Cambridge professors who received them showed no interest. They probably were too busy or too lazy to read them. But the third one took the time to really examine them and realized that what he was looking at was really mind-blowing.

This professor, whose name was G.H. Hardy, invited the young Indian boy to board a ship to the UK.

税务官看了看他的笔记本，发现这个年轻男子不仅擅长数学，而且极为聪明。他正在解答的数学难题也是顶级数学家们正在苦苦求解的问题。

如果一个没有受过多少教育的人——他至今的境遇不比乞丐好多少——能够在未受过训练的脑子里思考这些问题，他一定有一个惊人的大脑。

这位税务官没有给拉马努金提供一份税务局里的工作，而是推荐拉马努金为学术刊物撰写数学方面的文章。

但拉马努金需要赚钱维持生计，所以他不得不去做一些卑微的工作，只在闲暇时才撰写文章。这样的情况持续了很多年，直到另一个乐于助人的男子作出一项决定，把这位年轻男子得出的非凡方程式寄到他所认为的地球上最多聪明人的地方——英国的剑桥大学。

最先收到拉马努金方程式的两位剑桥大学教授对此没有任何兴趣。他们可能是太忙了，也可能是太懒了，所以根本没有看。但第三位教授花时间认真审读了这些公式，结果令他兴奋不已。

这位教授名叫哈代（G. H. Hardy），他邀请这位年轻的印度小伙子坐船去英国。

---

① **recommend** [rekə'mend] vt. 推荐、介绍、劝告、使受欢迎、托付；vi. 推荐、建议
② **extraordinary** [ɪk'strɔːdnrɪ] adj. 非凡的、特别的、离奇的、临时的、特派的
③ **equation** [ɪ'kweɪʒ(ə)n] n. 方程式、等式、相等，[化学]反应式

After much opposition from his penniless parents (and reluctance on his own part), he eventually travelled across the world and settled in the UK.

In Cambridge, it became obvious that Ramanujan was a rare genius. He wrote thousands of mathematical formulas. These were so amazing that other mathematicians studied them for years.

He was invited to join the Royal Society, which was a club for the world's top scientists.

But because of his poor background and the **malnutrition**[1] he had suffered, he was never healthy. He died in 1920, aged just 32 years old.

Recently, the Indian government declared that his birthday, December 22, be National Mathematics Day.

Today, all over the planet, people celebrate the genius of the poor boy with the amazing brain, and lament the fact that had the world been kinder to him, he might have achieved much more.

在经历身无分文的父母的反对以及自己内心的犹豫后,拉马努金最终选择跨越大半个地球到英国去,并且最后定居在那里。

在剑桥大学,拉马努金无疑是个罕见的天才。他得出了数千条数学公式,这些公式令人惊叹不已,其他数学家花了很多年时间来研究它们。

拉马努金受邀加入了世界上顶尖科学家云集的英国皇家学会。

然而,身世的卑微再加上从小营养不良,拉马努金的身体状况一直不太好。1920 年,拉马努金离开了人世,年仅 32 岁。

最近,印度政府宣布:将拉马努金的生日——12 月 22 日——定为国家数学日。

如今,全世界的人们都在纪念这位贫穷但拥有惊人头脑的天才男孩,同时也为他感到悲哀——如果世界对他友善一点,他可能会取得更多更大的成就。

① **malnutrition** [ˌmælnjʊˈtrɪʃ(ə)n] *n.* 营养失调、营养不良

THE GOOD WITCH WHO MADE AN AMAZING DECISION

玛丽亚·阿涅西
作出惊人决定的女巫

STEP C.

MARIA HAD A GREAT RELATIONSHIP with her father.

But then her parents had another child. And another. And another. And another. And another. And another. And so on — until the girl was eventually the eldest of 21 children!

How did Maria manage to keep his attention?

It was very, very hard — but she did it by being very, very brilliant. By the time she was 13 years old, she could speak Italian, French, Latin, Greek, German, Spanish and **Hebrew**[1].

And it wasn't just languages she was good at: she became a master of philosophy and mathematics. In those days, the 1700s, those were the top subjects at universities.

Her father, a professor, often invited other professors to their house in Italy to show off his clever oldest daughter.

But deep down, there was something wrong. Maria Agnesi's father liked to show off how super-smart his child was. But in her heart she did not value that type of knowledge. She was a quiet, **introverted**[2] girl who thought being kind and good-hearted was much more important than being clever.

Still, it seemed that **circumstances**[3] had made it important that she be seen as clever, so she did smart things.

玛丽亚和父亲的关系非常好。

但在她出生之后,母亲生了另一个孩子。接着又生了一个,接着又生了一个,接着又生了一个,接着又生了一个,接着又生了一个……玛丽亚最终成为 21 个孩子中年龄最大的!

玛丽亚该如何做,才能继续吸引父亲的注意呢?

要达到这个目的很难,但她做到了,因为她非常、非常聪明。13 岁时,她就掌握了意大利语、法语、拉丁语、希腊语、德语、西班牙语和希伯来语。

而且,她擅长的还不只是语言,她还成了哲学和数学名家。在她生活的 18 世纪,哲学和数学是大学中最顶尖的学科。

她的父亲是一名教授,经常邀请其他教授到他意大利的家中来做客,以炫耀他那聪明的长女。

※※※※

实际上这样做是不妥的。玛丽亚·阿涅西(Maria Agnesi)的父亲喜欢炫耀他的孩子有多聪明,但玛丽亚自己并不看重自己拥有的这种类型的知识。她是个安静、内向的女孩,她认为善良和仁慈比聪明更重要。

然而,环境要求玛丽亚成为世人眼中的聪明人,所以她不得不做一些聪明的事。

---

① **Hebrew** ['hi:bru:] *n.* 希伯来人、犹太人、希伯来语;*adj.* 希伯来语的、希伯来人的
② **introverted** ['ɪntrə(ʊ)vɜːtɪd] *adj.* (性格)内向的、内倾的、不爱交际的
③ **circumstance** ['sɜːkəmstəns] *n.* 环境、情况、事件、境遇

STEP C.

One of her great discoveries was a mathematics **formula**[1] which produced numbers to draw on graph paper, making a special type of curved (or turning) line. No one had ever made that formula before.

It was called the "**aversiera**[2]" which means "a turn" in Italian. But "aversiera" is also a short form for the similar word "avversiere", which means "wife of the devil" or "witch". So thanks to a translation mistake, her famous algebraic equation went down in history under the English name "the witch of Agnesi".

This was odd, because Maria Agnesi was the opposite of what we might think of as a witch. She was gentle and spiritual.

In 1750, Pope Benedict XIV appointed this brilliant young woman professor of science and mathematics at a university — which was extraordinary, since women in those days were not even allowed to be students, let alone professors.

她的重大发现之一是一个数学公式。利用这个公式演算得出某些数,然后在坐标纸上作图,能够构筑一条特殊类型的曲线。以前从未有人发现过这个公式。

作出的这条曲线被称为"箕舌线"(aversiera),意大利语的意思是"一道弯"。但"aversiera"这个词和"avversiere"很相似,而后者的意思是"恶魔的妻子"或"女巫"。所以由于翻译的错误,玛丽亚著名的代数公式在英语中以"阿涅西的女巫"之名流传下来。

这够古怪的,是吧?因为玛丽亚·阿涅西与我们想象的女巫的形象正好相反,她性情温和,品行高尚。

1750年,教皇本笃十四世任命玛丽亚——这位才华横溢的年轻女子——担任一所大学的科学和数学教授。这在当时是一项极不寻常举措,因为当时的女性甚至都不被允许作为学生去听课,更不要说成为教授了。

---

① **formula** ['fɔːmjʊlə] n. [数]公式、准则,配方,婴儿食品[formulas 或 formulae]
② **versiera** [vɛə'sjeərə] n. [数]箕舌线,意大利语中为 aversiera

But to everyone's amazement, Maria turned **down**[1] the job, and after her father died in 1752, she stopped doing mathematics and science completely.

This hyper-intelligent woman said that all her genius had taught her one extraordinary thing: that being good was more important than being clever.

She became a **nun**[2] and spent the rest of her life looking after the poor and the sick. She was buried with the **inmates**[3] of a home for penniless women when she died at the age of 81.

Some people thought it was a pity that such a clever woman had decided to drop her studies in science and mathematics.

But many people, when they thought about it, realized that with the choices she made, Maria had taught the whole world the most important lesson of all: perhaps life really is not about being rich and successful, but about being the person you were meant to be.

但令所有人吃惊的是,玛丽亚拒绝了这份工作。而且,在父亲于 1752 年去世后,她完全停止了数学和科学方面的研究。

这位聪明过人的女性说,她所有的天赋都在教导她做一件特别的事:做一个好人比做一个聪明的人更重要。

玛丽亚当了一名修女,将余生致力于照顾穷人和病人。她 81 岁去世,与收容所中穷困潦倒的女人们葬在一起。

有些人认为,这么聪明的一位女子决定放弃数学与科学研究是令人遗憾的。

但更多人在思考玛丽亚的这一行为时,却认识到,玛丽亚通过自己作出的这一选择,告诉了全世界一个最重要的道理:人生的意义也许不是成为一个富有、成功的人,而是成为一个自己想要成为的人。

① **turn down** 拒绝
② **nun** [nʌn] *n.* 修女、尼姑
③ **inmate** [ˈɪnmeɪt] *n.* (尤指)同院病人、同狱犯人、同被(收容所)收容者

THE STRANGE ADVENTURES OF DR. POISON

弗里德莱布·斐迪南·朗格
毒药博士的奇幻冒险

OOPS! A BOY AGED 15 accidentally **squirted**[1] poison into his eye. Uh-oh! This seemed like very bad news.

The young man's name was Friedlieb Ferdinand Runge, but that was hard to remember — so most people just called him F.F.

F.F. was helping his uncle in the laboratory, and was handling a plant called **henbane**[2]. Henbane has nothing to do with chickens, but comes from ancient words meaning "deadly poison".

He was trying to get the juice out of the plant when a bit of it squirted into his eye.

Good news: Not much went in, and he suffered no lasting damage.

But the even better news was that the boy, F.F., reacted like a scientist. He was fascinated. He wanted to record the data.

So he raced to a mirror and discovered that the little black disk in the middle of his eye had suddenly grown large.

Then it gradually **shrank**[3] back to the same size as the one in the other eye. Remarkable!

Friedlieb was born in Germany in 1794. After working with his uncle and having his happy accident he became a scientist (although there was no such word in those days, as the word "scientist" was coined in 1832).

哎呀！ 一个 15 岁的男孩不小心把毒药溅到自己的眼睛里了。啊哦！这看起来是个糟糕的消息。

这个小男孩名叫弗里德莱布·斐迪南·朗格（Friedlieb Ferdinand Runge），但这太难记了——所以大多数人直接叫他弗弗。

弗弗在实验室给他的叔叔帮忙，他正在处理一棵叫作 Henbane（天仙子）的植物。Henbane（天仙子）这个名字和鸡（Hen 是母鸡的意思）一点关系都没有，它源自古代意为"致命的毒药"的单词。

他竭尽全力从这株植物榨取汁液，几滴汁液飞溅到了眼中。

好消息是：溅进去的量不多，不会造成永久性伤害。

还有一个更好的消息是：小男孩弗弗的反应就像一名科学家一样，他着了迷似的想要记录下所发生的一切。

他跑到镜子面前，然后从镜中发现，溅进汁液的那只眼睛的瞳孔放大了。

接下来，瞳孔又逐渐收缩，恢复到与另一个正常的瞳孔一样大小。这太不寻常了！

❦

弗弗出生于 1794 年，是一名德国人。在同叔叔工作了一段时间，并且经历了那一次愉快的意外后，他成为一名科学家（尽管"科学家"这个词当时并不存在，直到 1832 年才被创造出来）。

---

① **squirt** [skwɜːt] *n.* 喷射、注射；*vt.* 喷射；*vi.* 喷出
② **henbane** ['henbeɪn] *n.* [植] 天仙子（野生毒草）、莨菪、茄科的药用植物
③ **shrink** [ʃrɪŋk] *n.* 收缩、畏缩；*vt.* 使缩小、使收缩；*vi.* 收缩、畏缩 [shrank, shrank, shrinking]

When F.F. was 25, he was quite well known at his university as a master of chemical analysis. His nickname was Doctor Poison, because he was fearless about doing experiments with chemicals that other people were scared of.

Living in the area was a very famous writer named Johann Wolfgang von Goethe, one of Europe's top literary **celebrities**[①].

Goethe wanted to meet Dr. Poison.

F.F. Runge, who was very poor, borrowed a smart black hat and a **frock**[②] coat, and took his cat with him, too.

He told Goethe all about how chemicals worked, and even put a drop of a chemical in the eye of his cat, to show how the pupil would grow large. (It didn't hurt the cat.)

Goethe was amazed.

He handed F.F. a little bag of beans which had been sent to him from Greece. People used the beans to make a marvelous drink called mocha coffee.

He gave the young man a challenge: What are the chemicals in this?

F.F. took the beans back to his lab and worked on them. He **deduced**[③] that the chemical that made coffee so popular was a white **crystalline**[④] substance hidden inside. He was right. We now call that chemical **caffeine**[⑤].

当弗弗 25 岁时,他作为一名化学分析能手,在他就读的大学中非常出名。他的外号是"毒药博士",因为他不会对其他人害怕的化学实验产生丝毫恐惧。

他家附近住着一位非常著名的作家,名字叫歌德(Johann Wolfgang von Goethe),他是欧洲顶尖的文学家之一。

歌德想要见见毒药博士。

朗格非常穷,他借了一顶漂亮的黑色帽子和一件男礼服大衣,还带上了他的猫,前去拜见歌德。

他告诉歌德化学品是如何生效的,甚至在身边那只猫的眼睛里滴了一滴化学物质,向歌德演示了一下瞳孔是如何扩张的(这并不会伤害到猫)。

歌德震惊了。

他给弗弗一包从希腊寄来的豆荚。当时的人们用这种豆荚调制一种口感极佳的饮品,叫作摩卡咖啡。

歌德向弗弗提出了一个挑战性的问题:这种豆荚里含有什么化学物质?

弗弗把豆荚带回了他的实验室,对它进行分析。他推断:使咖啡如此流行的化学物质是豆荚内部的一种白色结晶物。他是正确的,我们如今把这种物质称为咖啡因。

① **celebrity** [sɪ'lebrɪtɪ] *n.* 名人、名声 [celebrities]
② **frock** [frɒk] *n.* 女装、连衣裙、僧袍、罩袍
③ **deduce** [dɪ'djuːs] *vt.* 推论、推断、演绎出 [deduced, deduced, deducing]
④ **crystalline** ['krɪst(ə)laɪn] *adj.* 透明的、水晶般的、水晶制的、结晶的
⑤ **caffeine** ['kæfiːn] *n.* 咖啡因、茶精(兴奋剂)

F.F. Runge also developed paper **chromatography**[1], which is when you use a strip of paper which changes color to tell you important details about a liquid. This is used in **pregnancy**[2] tests and has many other uses.

When F.F. died, he was no longer called Dr. Poison. The newspaper announcement said: "After a brief illness, Dr. Friedlieb Ferdinand Runge, Professor of Technology, died this morning at six o'clock in his 74th year."

If your parents like to drink coffee, perhaps you can tell them about F.F., who went from being Dr. Poison to being Professor of Technology and discovered caffeine on the way.

弗弗还提出了纸层析法，这是一种通过纸带上颜色的改变来检验液体所含重要信息的方法。它被运用在验孕及其他许多方面。

弗弗去世后，他不再被称为毒药博士。报纸上的公告称："在短暂生病之后，弗里德莱布·斐迪南·朗格博士，科技教授，在今晨6点去世，享年74岁。"

如果你的父母喜欢喝咖啡，也许你可以告诉他们有关弗弗的故事：他从一名毒药博士变成了科技教授；从某种程度上来说，他还发现了咖啡因。

---

① **chromatography** [ˌkrəʊməˈtɒɡrəfɪ] *n.* 色层分析、色谱分析法
② **pregnancy** [ˈpreɡnənsɪ] *n.* 怀孕 [pregnancies]

THE YOUNG WOMAN WHO WAS FORGOTTEN

罗莎琳德·富兰克林
被遗忘的年轻女子

SCIENTISTS DISCOVERED THAT PEOPLE contain secret plans — instructions on how to build a human. It sounds strange, doesn't it, like a movie plot?

But it's true. Every cell in the human body contains molecules called DNA, which hold the information needed to make a person.

The full name of DNA is **Deoxyribonucleic Acid**[1], but that's hard to spell or say, even for scientists. So we all just say DNA.

Who discovered this? Quite a few people, but let's look at one of the contributors.

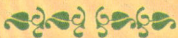

In 1950, Rosalind Franklin was 29 years old, and got a job working as a scientific researcher at a university laboratory in the UK.

She was clever, but some people found her to be rather a **grumpy**[2] person, and she definitely had a sharp **tongue**[3].

She worked with a man called Maurice Wilkins, who was the opposite: shy, polite and friendly. Sometimes people who are opposites fit together well, but not in this case. The two did not get on.

科学家发现，人们掌握着人类是如何被创造出来的秘密。这听起来很不可思议，就好像电影中的情节。是不是？

但这是真的，人体内的每一个细胞都包含着名叫 DNA 的分子，而这些分子蕴含着人体组成所需要的信息。

DNA 的全称叫脱氧核糖核酸，但这个词即使对科学家来说也太难拼写、太难读了，所以我们就直接叫它 DNA。

谁发现了 DNA 的结构？有好几个人都发现了，在这里让我们看看其中一位贡献者的故事。

1950 年，罗莎琳德·富兰克林（Rosalind Franklin）29 岁，她在英国一所大学的实验室中从事科研工作。

她很聪明，但有些人发现她脾气不太好，说话尖刻。

她与一位名叫莫里斯·威尔金斯（Maurice Wilkins）的男子一起工作，这位男子的脾气与她恰恰相反：他腼腆、有礼貌并且待人友善。有时脾气截然相反的两个人一起工作时正好互补，但在这里并不是这个样子：他们两人相处得并不融洽。

---

① Deoxyribonucleic Acid [diːˈɔksi,raibəunjuːˈkliːik] *n.* 脱氧核糖核酸
② grumpy [ˈgrʌmpɪ] *adj.* 脾气暴躁的、性情乖戾的；*n.* 脾气坏的人、爱抱怨的人 [grumpier, grumpiest]
③ tongue [tʌŋ] *n.* 舌头、语言

By 1953, scientists all knew that DNA existed, but nobody had ever seen it. It became a race to see who could find it first. (It was not a real race, of course, but scientists can be competitive, and they all wanted the glory of being the first to find something, and thus achieved **fame**①.)

At that time, Rosalind and Maurice were part of a team led by two highly **esteemed**② scientists, James Watson and Francis Crick.

One day, Rosalind, with one of her students (she worked at a university) used special cameras to try to take pictures of DNA.

This technique had never worked before. But this time, the result was a picture which was a rather **fuzzy**③ image with an odd shape in it. It was listed simply as "Photograph 51". The student took the picture with him to the office of the other scientist (the friendly one), Maurice Wilkins.

Then one of the project leaders, top scientist James Watson, came to Rosalind's room and warned that other scientists were close to finding the answer. He said that this team urgently needed to recheck their results if they were to have a chance of winning the race.

It seems that Rosalind may have thought that he was implying that she didn't know how to **interpret**④ her own data. Anyway, whatever she thought, the result was that she shouted at him!

1953 年，科学家都知道 DNA 的存在，但没有人见过它的结构。谁能够最先看到它就成了一项竞赛（当然，这并不是一项真正的比赛。但科学家都是具有竞争意识的，他们都想成为第一个发现者，获得这种荣誉就可扬名天下）。

当时罗莎琳德和莫里斯是同一个项目组的成员，这个项目组由两位颇负盛名的科学家——詹姆斯·沃森（James Watson）和弗朗西斯·克里克（Francis Crick）领导。

～～～～～

有一天，罗莎琳德（她在一所大学任教）和她的学生一起，试着利用特殊的照相技术拍摄 DNA 结构的照片。

之前他们使用这项技术从未得到想要的结果。但这次，相机拍摄到了一张相当模糊的照片，照片中的影像有着奇怪的形状。它被简单地标为"第 51 号照片"。一个学生拿着这张照片去了另一位科学家（友善的那位）——威尔金斯的办公室。

这时，项目组的领导之一、那位顶尖的科学家沃森，来到了罗莎琳德的房间。沃森提醒罗莎琳德，其他的科学家快要找到答案了。他说如果项目组想抓住机会赢得这场比赛，就亟须复核目前的成果。

罗莎琳德可能误解了他的意思，认为她不知道如何解释自己的研究数据。不管当时她是怎么想的，反正结果是，她对沃森大声咆哮起来！

----

① **fame** [feɪm] *n.* 名声、名望，传闻、传说
② **esteem** [ɪˈstiːm; e-] *vt.* 尊敬，认为、考虑，估价；*n.* 尊重、尊敬
③ **fuzzy** [ˈfʌzɪ] *adj.* 模糊的、失真的，有绒毛的 [fuzzier, fuzziest]
④ **interpret** [ɪnˈtɜːprɪt] *vt.* 说明、口译；*vi.* 解释、翻译

Watson backed out of the room — and **bumped**[1] straight into shy Maurice Wilkins, who had come to see what the noise was about.

Quiet, friendly Wilkins took Watson to his room and showed him Photograph 51.

The two top scientists, Watson and Crick, examined it carefully and worked out that DNA was a very odd molecule, like two ladders **braided**[2] together. They filled in all the details and published their results.

The two men became very famous and won the Nobel Prize.

Rosalind was forgotten. After her death, people discovered that it was she who led to the taking of the all-important Photograph 51. Had she been left out of the official reports because she was female? Or because she was hard to get on with? Or because her contribution had been quite small?

People have **debated**[3] these issues for a long time (and will surely continue to do so), but here we'll make no judgment, just taking one lesson from this **incident**[4].

It's always worth being friendly and likeable! Science is a team game, and being cooperative is really helpful.

沃森倒退着走出了罗莎琳德的房间——无意中一头撞到了腼腆的威尔金斯——威尔金斯想来看看发生喧哗的原因。

威尔金斯带着沃森去了他的房间，向他展示了第51号照片。

两位顶尖科学家——沃森和克里克仔细研究了这张照片，最后得出结论：DNA是一种非常古怪的分子，它的结构就如同两个纵横交错在一起的梯子。他们补充了所有的细节，并发表了这一最终结果。

这两名男子一下子出名了，并赢得了诺贝尔奖。

罗莎琳德被遗忘了。在她死后，人们才发现，正是她领导拍摄了这张非常重要的第51号照片。她之所以不被官方报道提及，是因为她是一名女性吗？还是因为她难以相处？还是因为她的贡献微乎其微？

人们对于这些问题争辩了很久（并肯定会继续争辩下去）。在这里我们对此不作评价，只是希望从这一事件中得出一些教训：

待人和善、讨人喜爱总是值得的！科研是一项团队工作，而具有合作精神非常有帮助。

① **bump** [bʌmp] n. 肿块、隆起物，撞击；vi. 碰撞、撞击，颠簸而行；vt. 碰、撞、颠簸
② **braid** [breɪd] vt. 编织；n. 辫子、穗带、发辫
③ **debate** [dɪˈbeɪt] vt. 辩论、争论、讨论；vi. 辩论、争论、讨论；n. 辩论、辩论会 [debated, debated, debating]
④ **incident** [ˈɪnsɪd(ə)nt] n. 事件、事变，插曲；adj.［光］入射的，附带的、易发生的、伴随而来的

THE GIRL IN THE CHAMBER OF CORPSES

亚历山德拉·吉莉安
停尸房里的女孩

PEOPLE WERE SCARED OF the natural philosopher and his chief assistant, despite the fact that he was a doctor and she was little more than a child.

That was because the **expertise**[1] of Dr Mondino de' Liuzzi and his young assistant Alessandra Giliani was cutting up dead bodies in the name of science.

People did not want to visit the place where they worked, because they worried that evil spirits **lurked**[2] there.

This fear made good scientific sense. Dead bodies soon rotted and if you touched them, you could easily get sick and die of invisible evil spirits, which we would now call **infectious**[3] viruses and bacteria.

Alessandra prepared **corpses**[4] for demonstrations and Dr. de' Liuzzi would show **audiences**[5] the internal organs of humans, explaining what they did.

The pair were creative, too.

Dr de' Liuzzi had an amazing way of **stitching**[6] together two thin pieces of **human tissue**[7]. He would hold the **flaps**[8] of skin together and get a large ant to bite them!

人们害怕一位自然哲学家和他的首席助理，尽管他是名医生，而他的助理不过是个小孩。

那是因为蒙迪诺·德·里尤兹（Mondino de' Liuzzi）医生和他的年轻助手亚历山德拉·吉莉安（Alessandra Giliani）的专长是以科学的名义解剖尸体。

人们不想到他们工作的地方去，因为担心那里埋伏着恶魔。

这种恐惧是有科学依据的。尸体会腐烂，如果你触碰他们，就很容易染病，死于不可见的恶魔。这种恶魔我们现在称之为传染性病毒和传染性细菌。

※※※※※※

亚历山德拉准备好用于展示的尸体，蒙迪诺医生则向观众展示人体内部的器官，解释它们的用途。

这对搭档也很有创意。

蒙迪诺医生能够用不可思议的方法将两片很薄的人体组织缝在一起。他会将皮瓣缝合在一起，然后让一只大蚂蚁咬开！

---

① **expertise** [ˌekspɜːˈtiːz] n. 专门知识、专门技术、专家的意见
② **lurk** [lɜːk] vi. 潜伏、潜藏、埋伏；n. 潜伏、埋伏
③ **infectious** [ɪnˈfekʃəs] adj. 传染的、传染性的、易传染的
④ **corpse** [kɔːps] n. 尸体
⑤ **audience** [ˈɔːdɪəns] n. 观众、听众、读者
⑥ **stitch** [stɪtʃ] n. 针脚、线迹，一针；vt. 缝、缝合；vi. 缝、缝合
⑦ **human tissue** 人体组织
⑧ **flap** [flæp] n. 片状垂下物、前襟、口袋盖、(帽)边、鞋舌、[航] 襟翼

Then he would kill the ant but leave the ant's head in place. He could stitch a wound together with a row of ants' heads.

Alessandra, a teenager, had also invented a new medical technique.

She had found a way of draining blood from a fresh dead body and replacing it with a dark liquid dye. That meant that you could see where the blood flowed through the human body.

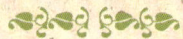

The scientist was quite successful and soon had a few other assistants. One of them, a young man named Otto, fell in love with Alessandra.

This happened in the early 1300s in Italy. The doctor wrote a book about all the parts of the human body and it became the most important book of anatomy for hundreds of years.

But what happened to Alessandra?

By the time she was 19, she and Otto had decided to get married.

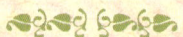

But then one day, after coming home from work, the young woman felt sick — very sick.

Alessandra had probably picked up an infection from one of the dead bodies. Today we have medicines called "**antibiotics**[1]" to **halt**[2] dangerous infections, but in those days poor Otto could do nothing.

接着，他把蚂蚁杀死，但留下蚂蚁的头。他能用一串蚂蚁的头颅缝合一个伤口！

亚历山德拉，一名十几岁的年轻人，也发明了一种新的医学技术。

她找到了一种方法，将刚去世之人体内的血液排空，然后代替以深色染料。这意味着我们可以看出血液在人体的哪些部位流动。

这位科学家非常成功，他很快就招收了其他一些助手，其中一名叫奥托（Otto）的年轻男子爱上了亚历山德拉。

这件事发生在 14 世纪早期的意大利。蒙迪诺医生写了一本关于人体所有部位的书，这本书也成为数百年内解剖学方面最重要的一本书。

但亚历山德拉怎么样了呢？

19 岁时，她决定和奥托结婚。

有一天下班回家后，她感觉到自己病了，而且病得非常厉害。

亚历山德拉很可能是被某具尸体感染了。今天我们有名为"抗生素"的药去阻断这种危险的感染，但在当时，她的丈夫、可怜的奥托什么也做不了。

---

① **antibiotics** [ˌæntɪbaɪˈɒtɪks] *n.* [药]抗生素、抗生学
② **halt** [hɔːlt] *vi.* 停止、立定、踌躇、犹豫；*n.* 停止、立定、休息；*vt.* 使停止、使立定

Alessandra died. It is believed that Otto put her remains in a pot and put a **plaque**[1] on it, saying: "In this **urn**[2], awaiting the **Resurrection**[3], are the mortal remains of Alessandra Giliani, young woman of Persiceto, **adept**[4] at anatomical demonstrations and unequalled disciple of the most famous doctor, Mondino de' Liuzzi."

There's not much information about her, so the details of her life come from guesswork.

But if she lived as we believe, then, 700 years ago, she gave her life to increase medical knowledge.

And today, if you get sick, related medical knowledge will make you well again. Maybe say a quick thank you to Alessandra, in case she is looking down on us!

亚历山德拉去世了。据说奥托把她的部分残骸放在一个罐子里埋了，并立了一块碑，上面写道："在这个坟墓里，亚历山德拉·吉莉安的凡人之躯正等待着复活。她是位来自佩尔西切托的姑娘，擅长解剖学演示，她是最著名的医生蒙迪诺·德·里尤兹最杰出的弟子。"

关于她的信息不多，所以她一生的细节都来自揣测。

如果她确实如我们所相信的那样，生活在 700 年前，她一定把自己的生命贡献给了提高人们的医学知识。

现在，如果你生病了，相关的医学知识会帮助你恢复健康。如果可能的话，向亚历山德拉表示感谢吧，说不定她正在天堂看着我们呢！

① **plaque** [plæk; plɑːk] *n.* 匾、血小板、饰板
② **urn** [ɜːn] *n.* 瓮、缸、茶水壶、坟墓、骨灰瓮
③ **resurrection** [ˌrezə'rekʃ(ə)n] *n.* 复活、恢复、复兴
④ **adept** [ə'dept; 'ædept] *adj.* 熟练的、擅长……的；*n.* 内行、能手

THE FARM GIRL WHO MADE YOUR MILK SAFE

爱丽丝·凯瑟琳·埃文斯
保证牛奶安全的农场姑娘

A FARM GIRL called Alice had a problem. She wanted to change the world, to make a difference, to leave her mark on humanity.

But what hope was there? She was a farm girl. And a poor one, at that time.

Worse still, she wasn't even healthy — as a small child, she and her brother **contracted**[1] a bad disease called **scarlet fever**[2], and only narrowly survived.

Alice Catherine Evans lived on a small farm in the countryside in Pennsylvania in the USA. Her parents did not earn enough money to send her to university, and besides, in those days, the late 1800s, girls were rarely encouraged to study.

When she left school, she took the only option available to her, becoming a teacher in a small town nearby.

Then one day, she heard that a famous university called Cornell University was offering free classes to poor **rural**[3] teachers.

She signed up and was soon studying bacteria, which many scientists believed were the cause of diseases like the one she had survived.

But it seemed that she could never escape her farming background.

一位叫爱丽丝的农场姑娘有点困扰。她想要改变世界,想要与众不同,想要在人类社会留下她自己的印记。

但可能吗?她是个农场姑娘,而且是个贫穷的农场姑娘。

更糟糕的是,她还体弱多病——还是小孩的时候,她和哥哥就感染了一种叫猩红热的大病,堪堪活了下来。

❦❦❦

爱丽丝·凯瑟琳·埃文斯(Alice Catherine Evans)住在美国宾夕法尼亚州乡下的一个小农场里。她的父母没有足够的钱供她上大学,而且在当时(19世纪末期),人们不鼓励女孩子读书学习。

离开学校后,她唯一的选择就是去附近的一个小镇当老师。

一天,她听到一个消息,说著名的康奈尔大学在为贫穷的乡村教师提供免费的课程。

她报了名,而且开始研究细菌。许多科学家认为,一些疾病——包括她曾感染的那场病的病因就是细菌。

但她似乎无法摆脱自己出身于农场这个背景。

---

① **contract** [ˈkɒntrækt] *vi.* 收缩、感染、订约;*vt.* 感染、订约、使缩短;*n.* 合同、婚约
② **scarlet fever** [内科]猩红热
③ **rural** [ˈrʊər(ə)l] *adj.* 农村的、乡下的、田园的、有乡村风味的

When she graduated and got a job, it was as a research scientist serving the dairy farm industry. Her **assignment**[1] was to improve the flavor of cheese.

One day, when she was in her early 30s, she had a thought, putting together the things she knew about: farms, bacteria and disease. There were several mysterious illnesses that humans had — could it be that they came from bacteria that caused diseases that people thought only cows got?

She went to her papers to take a look, and did some fresh research. Her studies showed a connection.

She tried to tell people with power about this. But they didn't listen: she was a woman, and they thought she didn't have enough qualifications to count as a real scientist. But a science journal published her claim in 1918.

Over the next few years, it became clear that she was right. Male scientists discovered the same thing — and plans were put in place to see what should be done.

Scientists knew that if you heated milk in a certain way, you would kill all the **germs**[2] in it while keeping the goodness of the milk unchanged. This was called **Pasteurization**[3], after the man who discovered it, Louis Pasteur.

Scientists used Alice Evans' findings to make a case for all milk to be processed in this way.

毕业后，她找到一份工作，以科研工作者的身份服务于乳制品工业。她的任务是改善奶酪的口味。

在她30多岁时，有一天，她产生了一个想法，把她所了解的农场、细菌和疾病联系到了一起：人们得一些神秘的疾病，这些疾病的产生有没有可能是因为某些细菌？是它们让人们患上以为只有奶牛才得的病？

她参照自己的论文并做了一些新的研究，研究结果显示疾病与细菌有某种关联。

她告诉人们这个结论，但大家丝毫不予理会，因为她是一个女人。而且他们认为，要被当作一名真正的科学家，她还不够格。不过在1918年，一本科学杂志发表了她的研究论文。

后来，她的说法被证明是正确的。男性科学家得出了相同的结果——并且制定了计划，看看应采取什么样的措施。

科学家发现，如果以一种特定的方式加热牛奶，能够在保证牛奶的营养成分不流失的同时杀死所有的细菌。这种操作被称为巴氏杀菌法，名字取自发明这种方法的人——路易斯·巴斯德（Louis Pasteur）。

科学家利用埃文斯的发现，为人们以这种方式处理牛奶提供了足够的理论依据。

---

① **assignment** [əˈsaɪnm(ə)nt] *n.* 分配、任务，作业，功课
② **germ** [dʒɜːm] *n.* [植]胚芽、萌芽，细菌；*vi.* 萌芽
③ **Pasteurization** [ˌpæstəraɪˈzeɪʃn] *n.* 加热杀菌法、巴斯德氏杀菌法

Today, if you go to your local store, whether it is in Singapore, or New York, or Nairobi, you will almost definitely find words such as "Pasteurized" printed in small letters on the carton. And you can drink it knowing that it will do you no harm.

And it's all because a farm girl called Alice, who wanted to make a difference in the world, succeeded in doing just that. In every area of interest, there are discoveries to be made. So, what are you interested in?

如今，无论是在新加坡、纽约还是内罗毕……如果你去超市，几乎可以肯定的是，你会在牛奶纸盒上找到用小字体印刷的"巴氏杀菌"几个字。这种牛奶你可以喝，因为它对你完全无害。

这都源自一位名叫爱丽丝的农场姑娘，她想要对世界作出些改变，并且真的做到了。只要兴趣所及，就能发现新的事物。所以，你对什么感兴趣呢？

A TASTY TREAT FOUND BY ACCIDENT

弗兰克·埃珀森
偶然发现的美味食品

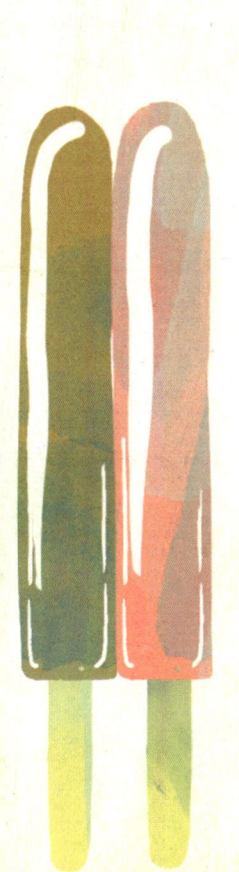
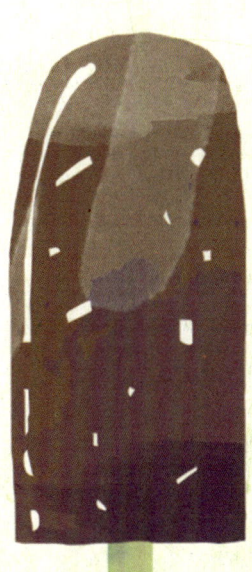

DO YOU LOVE FROZEN SNACKS? Most young people love **popsicles**①, also known as ice **lollies**② or ice pops.

These are pieces of fruit-flavored sugar-ice on a stick, sometimes with multi-colored sections or sweet bits added.

Most foods these days are invented by chefs working in kitchens belonging to restaurants or to big corporations. But in the past, foods were invented by ordinary people.

Frank Epperson was only about 11 years old when he accidentally invented popsicles, in 1905. In those days, the only frozen dessert known to most people was ice cream.

Frank wasn't trying to make a dessert, or any type of food. He was just thirsty. You couldn't buy a carton of real juice then— if you wanted a sweet drink, you bought oranges and **squeezed**③ them. If you could not afford to do that, you stirred fruit-flavored powder into a glass of tap water.

One cold night, the boy was stirring such a drink and stepped out of the house, and put the glass down for a moment. But then he forgot all about it and went inside and put himself to bed without thinking about his drink.

The next morning he stepped outside and found that the drink had frozen solid. He pulled the stirring stick upwards and the drink came with it — it kept its shape, looking like a huge, brightly colored ice-cube. Out of curiosity, he licked it and found it tasted good.

你喜欢冰冻的零食吗？大多数年轻人喜欢棒冰，它有时也被称为冰棒棒糖或是冰饮料。

棒冰是插在一根棒上的块状水果味冰糖，有时候其中会添加一些彩色的或者甜的杂食。

如今大多数的食物都是由在饭店或者大公司中工作的主厨发明的，但在过去，食物是由普通老百姓发明的。

&&&&&&&&&

1905年，当弗兰克·埃珀森（Frank Epperson）无意中发明棒冰时，他年仅11岁。在那时，冰激凌是大多数人知道的唯一的冰冻甜品。

弗兰克的本意并不在于制作一份甜品，他也不想要制作任何食物，他只是渴了。在那时，当你想喝一些甜的饮品时，你无法直接买到一盒真果汁。你得买橙子，然后自己榨汁。如果你买不起橙子，那就只能把水果味的粉末倒进一杯饮用水中，自己调一杯饮料喝。

一个寒冷的夜晚，这个男孩调制了一杯这样的饮料。他走出屋子，把杯子在屋外放了一会。然后他完全忘记了这件事，回到屋子里睡觉了。

第二天早上他走出屋子，发现那杯饮料已经被冻成了固体。他把搅拌棒连同饮品一起从杯子里拔了出来——它保持着一杯水的形状，看起来就好像一个巨大的、色彩斑斓的冰冻立方体。出于好奇心，他舔了一下，发现很好吃。

---

① **popsicle**［ˈpɑpsɪkl］*n.* 棒冰（商标名）
② **lolly**［ˈlɒlɪ］*n.* 棒棒糖［lollies］
③ **squeeze**［skwiːz］*vt.* 挤、紧握，勒索；*vi.* 压榨；*n.* 压榨、紧握、拥挤、佣金［squeezed，squeezed，squeezing］

And then he forgot all about it.

Seventeen years later it popped back into his mind. He was helping to **cater**① for a firemen's ball in his home city, which was Oakland, in California, in the USA.

He made a large **batch**② of frozen drinks to **lick**③ and served them to the party-goers, who loved them. The following year, he sold the "frozen lollipops" as snacks at an amusement park, and realized that this was a good idea for a business. They were cheap and easy to make, and quite profitable. They were just made from tap water and a bit of sweetened, fruit-flavored powder.

In 1923, Frank Epperson took out a patent, which is a document **certifying**④ that you have invented something new, and started selling them.

He wanted to call them epsicles, but he had children of his own then, and they preferred the name popsicles. Their choice stuck, especially when a New York company started mass-producing them under that name. One of the meanings of the word "pop" is "sweet drink" and the other part of the word comes from "icicle".

These days you can buy popsicles (or ice lollies) all over the world in flavors of fruit or chocolate or even green tea.

One of the reasons children love them so much is that they often change the color of your tongue for a while. Eat a blue popsicle and then stick your tongue out in front of a mirror — it's a pretty funny sight!

然后他又完全忘记了这件事。

17 年后，弗兰克回想起了这件事。当时他正待在家乡，为美国加利福尼亚州奥克兰市的一场消防员舞会准备食物。

他制作了一批可以舔着吃的冰冻饮品，提供给派对参加者。他们都很喜欢。接下来的几年，他在一所游乐园中把"冰冻棒棒糖"作为零食销售，逐渐意识到这里面的商机。这种食物又便宜又易于制作，还能带来很大的收益。它的原材料只不过是饮用水和一些甜的水果味粉末。

1923 年，弗兰克·埃珀森注册了专利（专利是一种证明文件，证明某人发明了某样新东西），证明是他发明了这种新式食品，并开始销售。

他想将这种食物取名为 epsicle，但他的孩子们更想把它取名为 popsicle。孩子们的选择胜出，并流传开来，特别是当一家纽约公司以这个名称开始大量生产这种食物后。现在这个名字（popsicle）中的"pop"，含义是"甜味饮品"，名字的其他部分（icicle）意思是"冰柱"。

如今，你可以在全世界范围内买到水果味、巧克力味甚至是绿茶味的棒冰（或是冰棒棒糖）。

孩子们如此喜爱它的原因之一是：它们能够暂时性地改变你舌头的颜色。当你吃着一根蓝色的棒冰，并在镜子前伸出你的舌头——这是多么有趣的画面啊！

---

① **cater** ['keɪtə] *vt.* 投合、迎合、满足需要，提供饮食及服务
② **batch** [bætʃ] *n.* 一批、一炉、一次所制之量；*vt.* 分批处理
③ **lick** [lɪk] *vt.* 舔，鞭打；*vi.* 舔、轻轻拍打
④ **certify** ['sɜːtɪfaɪ] *v.* 证明、保证 [certified, certified, certifying]

The Young Scientists Series:
Magical Mathematics and Advances in Alchemy

by

Nury Vittachi

English Copyright © 2017 by World Scientific Publishing Co. Pte. Ltd.

Bi-lingual (Simplified Chinese & English) Character Copyright © 2018 by Shanghai Scientific & Technological Education Publishing House

Shanghai Scientific & Technological Education Publishing House published bi-lingual edition by arranged with World Scientific Publishing Co. Pte. Ltd., Singapore

All rights reserved. This book, or parts thereof, may not be reproduced in any form or by any means, electronic or mechanical, including photocopying, recording or any information storage and retrieval system now known or to be invented, without written permission from the Publisher.

ALL RIGHTS RESERVED

上海科技教育出版社业经World Scientific Publishing Co. Pte. Ltd.同意取得本书中英文双语版版权

责任编辑　侯慧菊
封面设计　杨　静

"伟人的少年故事"丛书
迷人的科学——用思想创造奇迹的科学家
［斯里兰卡］努雷·维塔奇（Nury Vittachi）　著
斯泰帕·张（Step Cheung）　图
朱之翀　译
张　群　审校

出版发行	上海科技教育出版社有限公司
	（上海市柳州路218号　邮政编码200235）
网　址	www.ewen.co　www.sste.com
经　销	各地新华书店
印　刷	上海昌鑫龙印务有限公司
开　本	889×1194　1/32
印　张	3
版　次	2018年8月第1版
印　次	2018年8月第1次印刷
书　号	ISBN 978-7-5428-6712-4/G·3838
图　字	09-2017-937号
定　价	25.00元

扫描二维码
获取教师参考资料
及练习答案

扫描二维码
获取学生练习册